"I have walked that long road to freedom. . . . But I can rest only for a moment, for with freedom come responsibilities, and I dare not linger, for my long walk is not yet ended."

—NELSON MANDELA

NELSON MANDELA: ACTIVIST FOR EQUALITY

BY ROBERT GREEN

The Child's World

Published in the United States of America by The Child's World®
PO Box 326
Chanhassen, MN 55317-0326
800-599-READ
www.childsworld.com

The Child's World®: Mary Berendes, Publishing Director
Editorial Directions, Inc.: E. Russell Primm, Emily Dolbear, Lucia Raatma
and Sarah E. De Capua, Editors; Linda S. Koutris, Photo Selector; Alice Flanagan,
Photo Research; Red Line Editorial, Fact Research; Tim Griffin/IndexServ, Indexer;
Melissa McDaniel, Proofreader

Cover photograph: Portrait of Nelson Mandela/ © David Turnley/Corbis

Interior photographs ©: AP/Wide World Photos: 14, 16, 23; Obed Zilwa/AP/Wide World Photos: 6;
Jurgen Schadeberg/AP/Wide World Photos: 17, 19; Bob Gosani/AP/Wide World Photos: 22; John
Parkin/AP/Wide World Photos: 30, 34; Jon Eeg/AP/Wide World Photos: 31; Denis Farrell/AP/Wide World
Photos: 33; Themba Hadebe/AP/Wide World Photos: 36; Corbis: 11, 13; David Turnley/Corbis: 2;
Hulton-Deutsch Collection/Corbis: 7, 10; Roger De La Harpe, Gallo Images/Corbis: 8; Inge Yspeert/Corbis:
12; Bettmann/Corbis: 18, 20, 25; Hulton Archive/Getty Images: 21, 24, 28; Reuters/Hulton Archive/Getty
Images: 26; Louise Gubb/Newsmakers/Getty Images: 27; Jason Lauré: 15.

Library of Congress Cataloging-in-Publication Data
Nelson Mandela : activist for equality / by Robert Green.
p. cm. — (Journey to freedom)
Summary: A biography of the South African leader who became a civil rights activist, political prisoner, and
president of South Africa. Includes bibliographical references and index.
ISBN 1-56766-648-5 (lib. bdg. : alk. paper)
1. Mandela, Nelson, 1918– —Juvenile literature. 2. Presidents—South Africa—Biography—Juvenile literature.
[1. Mandela, Nelson, 1918– 2. Presidents—South Africa. 3. Civil rights workers. 4. Nobel Prizes—Biography.
5. Blacks—South Africa—Biography.] I. Title. II. Series.
DT1974 .G75 2002
968.06'5'092—dc21
2001007941

Contents

The Son of a Tembu Royal 7

Joining the Fight 14

Spear of the Nation 20

Hope and Glory 25

Timeline 37

Glossary 38

Index 39

Further Information 40

NELSON MANDELA HELPED CHANGE SOUTH AFRICA BY STANDING UP TO AN UNJUST GOVERNMENT. HIS COURAGE INSPIRED THE WORLD.

The Son of a Tembu Royal

On July 18, 1918, in the town of Umtata, a Tembu tribal chief's son was born. He was given the name Rolihlahla, a word from the Xhosa language meaning "pulling the branch of a tree"—a clever description for a "troublemaker." Rolihlahla Mandela would later be called Nelson.

In later years, the friends of Nelson Rolihlahla Mandela made much of his Tembu name. They took it as an omen of the role Mandela would play in bringing down the **racist** government of South Africa. This role earned him the gratitude of his people and the admiration of the world.

Nelson Mandela grew up in a village on a bank of the Mbashe River, in the area known as Tembuland, one of the ancient kingdoms of southern Africa. Long before South Africa was founded, the Tembu chiefs ruled this part of Africa. At that time, South Africa was a series of tribal regions, each with its own local language, and customs.

TRIBAL CHIEFS AND WITCH DOCTORS IN SOUTH AFRICA. MANDELA WAS BORN INTO THE TEMBU TRIBE AND WAS INFLUENCED BY THEIR RICH CULTURE.

A GIRAFFE IN ZWAZULU NATIONAL PARK. SOUTH AFRICA BOASTS PLENTIFUL GRASSLANDS AND A WIDE VARIETY OF WILDLIFE.

Nelson lived with his parents and other relatives in a small cluster of beehive-shaped huts. Tembu life was simple. The huts were made of field grasses and mud, the floors were earthen, and meals were cooked on open fires. The primary wealth of the Tembu came from the cattle they herded on the grasslands called the **veld**.

As a child, Nelson spent most of his time outside. His playground was the great veld surrounding the village. His toys were animals made of wet clay and weapons made of straight, strong tree branches.

Stick-fighting was one of his favorite games. The children imitated the great warriors of the Tembu tribe. Although Nelson's life was simple in terms of physical objects, it was rich in **folklore** and tradition.

Nelson loved to listen to the Tembu elders talk of the greatness of the kingdom. He learned the tribe's history and system of beliefs from the mouths of the elders, not from books. Very few people in his village knew how to read or write. Even his father, who was a member of the Tembu royal family and a councilor to their king, could not read.

Nelson's father had no formal education, but he took the advice of two friends and sent his son to school. Nelson's education was patterned after a British education. Students were taught in English. On the first day of school, his teacher gave him the name Nelson.

An open-air schoolhouse near Johannesburg. Mandela attended a modest school like this one and was taught about South Africa as well as other countries.

In the one-room schoolhouse, Miss Mdingane taught Nelson to spell out English words in chalk on a black slate. She taught him geography and history. And Nelson learned that Great Britain had a vast empire that stretched around the globe. South Africa was one of Great Britain's colonies, and the rulers of South Africa were white people from Britain. In these early days, young Nelson had seen white men only occasionally. The local **magistrates** were white, and Nelson sometimes passed them on the street or saw them riding on horseback. Nelson also saw European missionaries who had come to South Africa.

MAGISTRATES IN THE TOWN OF LADYSMITH. FOR MANY YEARS, SOUTH AFRICA WAS GOVERNED BY WHITE MEN, INCLUDING OFFICIALS FROM GREAT BRITAIN.

Because the government was controlled by white Christians, many Africans, hoping to get ahead, converted to Christianity. Nelson had a good opinion of the Christians who ruled South Africa, so he decided to join the Methodist Church and become Christian. He also believed that whites had done many positive things for Africans, such as teaching them to write, building roads, and enforcing the law through their policemen and in courts of law.

When he was sixteen years old, Nelson passed through a traditional ceremony signaling the end of his childhood. That day, the first day of his adult life, one of the chiefs spoke, and his words startled Nelson.

A Xhosa boy during his initiation rite. Mandela experienced a similar tribal ceremony, which marked the end of his childhood.

The chief said that the black people of South Africa were slaves in their own country. White men ruled them and gave them no freedom. The whites, he said, used black Africans only to dig in the gold mines, and the wealth of their land passed into the hands of these white people. The chief said that English laws existed only to protect the white rulers.

Nelson was bitter that day. He had always considered white men a natural part of South Africa. Now, for the first time, he wondered why the whites were there and why the chiefs were unhappy about it.

MANY BLACK AFRICANS WORKED LONG, HARD DAYS IN THE COUNTRY'S GOLD MINES. BUT THESE MINES MADE ONLY THE WHITE CITIZENS RICH.

Joining the Fight

The white rulers of South Africa were sometimes referred to as the "the white tribe of Africa," but they were not from Africa at all. They were Europeans from Great Britain, Holland, France, and other countries.

The two largest groups were the British and the **Dutch.** At the time Mandela was born, South Africa was part of the British Empire. Thus, Mandela received an English education at school.

By the time he entered the University College of Fort Hare, one of the few black colleges in South Africa, Mandela prided himself on his English dress and manners. University students such as Mandela were often called "the black Englishmen," because they behaved more like the English than most Africans.

THE CITY OF JOHANNESBURG IN THE PROVINCE OF TRANSVAAL. MANDELA'S LIFE CHANGED DRAMATICALLY WHEN HE MOVED TO THIS CITY.

While Nelson Mandela was on summer vacation from college, his tribal elders decided that he should marry. Mandela preferred to choose his own wife, however, so he ignored the elders' wishes and ran away. He and a friend decided to go to Johannesburg, a large city located in the northern province of Transvaal.

In Johannesburg, Mandela received another kind of education. He was introduced to a successful businessman and community leader named Walter Sisulu. Sisulu changed Mandela's life dramatically, and the two became great friends. Sisulu got Mandela a job as a law clerk. In South Africa in those days, working in a law office was quite unusual for a black man.

STUDENTS AT WITWATERSRAND UNIVERSITY. MANDELA STUDIED THE LAW THROUGH COURSES OFFERED AT THE SCHOOL.

WALTER SISULU (CENTER), A SUCCESSFUL BUSINESSMAN AND COMMUNITY LEADER, PLAYED A KEY ROLE IN MANDELA'S LIFE. HE HELPED MANDELA GET A JOB AS A LAW CLERK, AND THE TWO MEN BECAME GOOD FRIENDS.

Nelson also started studying law through the mail at Johannesburg's Witwatersrand University. Studying law allowed Mandela to understand the thousands of rules and regulations limiting the lives of black Africans in their own country. His own Tembu society prized the open discussion of ideas and problems. He believed the traditional African societies prized democracy and fairness.

As he studied the white man's laws, Mandela found a devotion to equality and fairness in the spirit of the law. In principle, everyone was equal under the law. A person who broke the law was a criminal, no matter how great his or her wealth or what color his or her skin was. But the laws in South Africa were not fair laws. There was one set of laws for whites and another set for blacks. Mandela was becoming aware of the injustice of South African law.

MANDELA STUDIED HARD TO LEARN THE LAWS OF SOUTH AFRICA. THEN HE COMMITTED HIMSELF TO MAKING THOSE LAWS FAIR FOR EVERYONE.

Through Sisulu and other friends in Johannesburg, Mandela met fellow black Africans who were fighting against these unjust laws. He attended meetings of the African National Congress (ANC), an organization that worked to end discrimination. The organization elected him president of its youth league. Nelson had decided to join the struggle against the government that denied nonwhite South Africans their rights.

One way that Mandela intended to fight the government was through the law courts. In 1952, he and a college friend named Oliver Tambo opened South Africa's first black law practice. Within a short time, they had a flood of clients.

OLIVER TAMBO IN THE 1960s. TAMBO MET MANDELA WHILE THEY BOTH WERE ATTENDING THE UNIVERSITY COLLEGE OF FORT HARE, AND THEY LATER OPENED A LAW FIRM TOGETHER.

The laws restricting blacks were many, and it was easy to break one of these laws. For example, one might forget one's Native pass, which were identity papers, or mistakenly enter a "white's only" business, or travel without permission. At the offices of Mandela and Tambo Attorneys at Law, however, black citizens got sympathetic support. Mandela spent long days representing clients in court and evenings meeting with ANC members. Somehow he also had time to get married and start a family. But his life was so hectic that Mandela's son once asked his mother, "Where does daddy live?"

NELSON MANDELA AT HIS LAW FIRM. HE WORKED LONG HOURS AND LED A BUSY LIFE AS AN ATTORNEY, OFTEN NEGLECTING FAMILY RESPONSIBILITIES.

Spear of the Nation

Just as Mandela's resolve to fight the South African government was hardening, the government itself changed. In 1948, four years before Mandela opened his law practice, the Nationalist Party of South Africa was voted into power. The Nationalist Party represented the Afrikaners, or Dutch South Africans. It was the first South African government in which the British lost the majority.

The new government passed a series of laws known as **apartheid** laws. *Apartheid* means "apart" in Afrikaner, the language of Dutch South Africans. Discrimination against blacks, the large Indian population, and people of mixed racial background was now a national law. Overnight, the struggle of the ANC had become much more difficult—and much more dangerous.

PRIME MINISTER DANIEL F. MALAN IN 1948, THE YEAR THAT THE NATIONALIST PARTY WAS VOTED INTO POWER. THAT POLITICAL PARTY REPRESENTED SOUTH AFRICA'S AFRIKANERS.

In 1956, Mandela was arrested after organizing a peaceful protest against the South African government. He was accused of threatening to overthrow the government. This was a very serious charge, one that carried a maximum penalty of death. While the government prepared the case against Mandela and his lawyers prepared his defense, he was released on parole. This meant that he could go free while the court trials proceeded.

While he was on parole, Mandela could not leave Johannesburg, but he could continue to practice law. He spent much time preparing for his legal fight while also doing his ANC work. He continued to organize demonstrations and protests, even with the court case hanging over his head.

A BLACK AFRICAN BEING STOPPED BY A POLICEMAN. REGULAR CHECKS OF NATIVE PASSES WERE COMMONPLACE IN SOUTH AFRICA DURING APARTHEID.

WHILE HE WAS ON TRIAL FOR TRYING TO OVERTHROW THE GOVERNMENT, MANDELA (LEFT) PREPARED HIS LEGAL FIGHT AND CONTINUED TO PRACTICE LAW. HE ALSO FOUND TIME FOR PHYSICAL ACTIVITY.

In 1961, five years after he had been arrested, the court finally reached a decision. ANC members, newspaper reporters, and Mandela's relatives crowded into the courthouse that day. When the judge announced that there was not enough evidence to convict Mandela, the spectators erupted with cheers and singing. Mandela was not so happy.

Although he was found innocent, he believed that the police would find another reason to arrest him. His faith in the legal system was weakening. He had seen too many times that the law would not protect black Africans. In fact, it was through the apartheid laws that whites oppressed black Africans.

Mandela had always favored peaceful demonstrations against the government. After repeatedly seeing peaceful protests violently crushed by the police, however, he began to see no alternative to a violent struggle with the government.

BY 1961, MANDELA WAS FOUND
INNOCENT OF TRYING TO
OVERTHROW THE GOVERNMENT.
HIS FAITH THE LEGAL SYSTEM
HAD WEAKENED, HOWEVER, AND
HE BEGAN TO CONSIDER OTHER
WAYS TO FIGHT INJUSTICE IN
SOUTH AFRICA.

He became the leader of a new organization that planned to use violence against the white government. This group was called the Spear of the Nation. Mandela was the tip of that spear. Like his Tembu ancestors, he was now a warrior fighting to protect the rights of his people. "At a certain point," he wrote, "one can only fight fire with fire."

He knew that if he were caught, there would be no hope of winning another trial. He went underground, living like a fugitive. He let his hair grow longer and dressed in coveralls to disguise himself as a workman. He moved from place to place. He worked mostly at night and rarely left the house in the daylight. He decided to attack the government by blowing up government buildings. He chose this method, known as **sabotage**, hoping to destroy empty buildings rather than injure people.

After the Spear of the Nation set off its first bombs, the government began to hunt Mandela. For eight months, he lived on the run. Police searched for him everywhere and finally he was arrested. He was charged with high treason and trying to violently overthrow the government.

At his trial, he explained that he was fighting against racism, whether it was against black men or white men. He was sentenced to life in prison and sent to the jail on Robben Island near the coastal city of Cape Town. A new kind of struggle was just beginning—the struggle against the endless misery of prison life and the struggle against the despair.

Hope and Glory

Life in prison was harsh. The food was terrible, the cells were tiny, and the guards were often cruel. Even newspapers were forbidden. To get news of the outside world and the ANC struggle, prisoners paid the guards to smuggle in newspapers. Prisoners leaving the jail smuggled out information to Mandela's wife and the ANC leaders.

ANTI-APARTHEID ACTIVIST ROBERT SOBUKWE AT ROBBEN ISLAND. IT WAS IN A CELL LIKE THIS ONE THAT MANDELA SPENT DECADES OF HIS LIFE.

Mandela had grown apart from his first wife and the two had divorced. In 1958, while still on trial, he married again. Mandela's second wife, Winnie, would be his link to the outside world for the twenty-seven years he spent in prison. She was South Africa's first black professional social welfare worker. Her struggles against poverty and the other problems facing black South Africans led her to support the ANC and Mandela's work.

They spent only a few years together before Mandela was sent to prison, but Winnie Mandela proved to be Nelson's greatest supporter. She tirelessly kept her husband's memory alive. And her success was just as great outside South Africa.

WINNIE MANDELA WITH NELSON'S PHOTOGRAPH. EVEN WHILE THEY WERE APART ALL THOSE YEARS, WINNIE MANDELA KEPT HER HUSBAND IN HER THOUGHTS AND REMAINED HIS LINK TO THE OUTSIDE WORLD.

ANTI-APARTHEID ACTIVISTS IN ENGLAND. BY HOLDING DEMONSTRATIONS AND BOYCOTTING BUSINESSES, PEOPLE ALL OVER THE WORLD REACTED TO THE UNJUST LAWS OF SOUTH AFRICA.

After the Nationalist Party had adopted the apartheid laws, other countries looked on South Africa as a racist nation. Through Winnie's Mandela's efforts, Nelson Mandela became a symbol of the suffering of black South Africans. Foreign newspaper reporters wrote columns about him. He became a folk hero for many civil rights groups throughout the world. Everywhere, songs and posters carried the slogan, "Free Nelson Mandela."

Mandela heard only rumors of this. He was frequently kept in solitary confinement, spending his days in a tiny cell and being allowed only thirty minutes of exercise each day. These were lonely days. He lived on hope in the belief that his sacrifice was for the good of South Africa.

In 1984, Mandela was transferred to Pollsmoor Prison near Cape Town, and four years later, he was taken to the Victor Verster Prison near Paarl. Sometimes he was allowed to work with other prisoners. He harvested seaweed and quarried limestone. He often worked alongside other imprisoned members of the ANC. He led protests even in prison. Through hunger strikes, he managed to have the prison food improved a little.

By the late 1980s, foreign governments and companies were **boycotting** business with South Africa. Some even broke off diplomatic relations. South Africa grew poorer and more isolated. Black Africans, strengthened by the support they had witnessed from foreign countries, continued their strikes and protests.

PRESIDENT F. W. DE KLERK BEING SWORN IN AS PRESIDENT OF SOUTH AFRICA. DE KLERK RECOGNIZED THE PROBLEMS OF APARTHEID AND WORKED TO CHANGE HIS GOVERNMENT.

President F. W. de Klerk, who served South Africa from 1989 to 1994, ruled a country headed toward disaster. The Nationalist Party's efforts to keep South Africa's white government in power began to destroy the country. President de Klerk realized that his country could not continue on its current course.

In February 1990, de Klerk announced radical changes. He was going to **dismantle** apartheid and allow the ANC to become a legal political party. A few days later, he summoned Nelson Mandela to his office. De Klerk greeted Mandela with a handshake and told him that he would be released from prison the following day.

Nelson Mandela was startled. For nearly thirty years, prison had been his home. President de Klerk was stunned when Mandela told him that he needed a little time to plan things. De Klerk was telling a prisoner that he could go free, and the prisoner was asking for a little more time in jail. That meeting was an odd beginning to their relationship.

These two men, one representing black South Africans and one representing the white government, eventually worked together for all of South Africa. It took a great deal of bravery on both sides. Mandela had spent half his life in prison for his struggle. De Klerk faced the wrath of white South Africans who felt betrayed. Before their work was done, the two leaders were awarded the 1993 Nobel Peace Prize.

NELSON MANDELA AND F. W. DE KLERK AT THE NOBEL PEACE PRIZE CEREMONY. THESE TWO MEN WERE HONORED WITH THIS AWARD IN 1993.

Once he was out of prison, Mandela realized just how much the world had changed. He was greeted everywhere as a celebrity. As the head of the ANC, Mandela traveled to Europe and the United States. People cheered him everywhere he went. All those years of feeling isolated and alone in prison had not been wasted. He had become a silent symbol. Now free to speak, Mandela was happy that people were listening. Even the South African government was listening!

With de Klerk, he worked out new rights for black Africans. They were allowed to vote in the next election, to own land, and to travel freely. In short, black Africans were to be equal citizens.

When the polls opened on April 27, 1994, blacks lined up all over the country to vote. Sometimes they had to wait for hours. In line, they danced and sang. It was a joyous day. When the voting was completed, an emotional former prisoner of the white South African government discovered that he had been elected president. The ANC, once a criminal organization, had replaced the Nationalist Party and formed the first black government of the country of South Africa.

WHEN THE POLLS OPENED IN SOUTH AFRICA ON APRIL 27, 1994, THE LINES WERE VERY LONG. BUT BLACK AFRICANS EMBRACED THEIR RIGHT TO VOTE AND DIDN'T MIND WAITING FOR HOURS TO CAST THEIR BALLOTS.

NELSON MANDELA ON THE DAY OF HIS INAUGURATION AS PRESIDENT OF SOUTH AFRICA. MANDELA SERVED FROM 1994 TO 1999, AND TODAY HE CONTINUES IN HIS EFFORTS TO MAKE HIS COUNTRY A BETTER PLACE.

Mandela served as president of South Africa for five years. It was a busy time. Apartheid had to be dismantled. The constitution and all the other laws governing people's lives had to be rewritten. Diplomatic relations had to be reestablished with other countries. And the past had to be dealt with.

Mandela did not want the whites of South Africa to flee the country. He did everything he could to protect them from revenge. He won international recognition for making a smooth and peaceful transition to a black majority government. He proved, above all, that he could do more than simply oppose an unjust government—he could also run a just government.

When his term expired, Mandela longed to return to a quieter life. He had missed out on too many things in prison. He wanted to see his children, whom he hardly knew. He also discovered that he and his wife, Winnie, had both changed. They decided to separate. He married for a third time in 1998. His new wife, Graca Machel, was the widow of President Somora Machel of Mozambique.

Since retiring from politics, Mandela has continued to work for a better South Africa. He has campaigned as a private citizen for the protection of the natural environment and led campaigns to increase the awareness of the disease acquired immunodeficiency syndrome (AIDS). Over the years, Mandela has received honorary degrees from more than fifty international universities. He sacrificed much of his life for a better South Africa, and to this day he still struggles in the name of all South Africans.

NELSON MANDELA AND HIS THIRD WIFE, GRACA MACHEL, WERE MARRIED IN 1998. SHE IS THE WIDOW OF A MOZAMBIQUE PRESIDENT.

Timeline

1918	Nelson Mandela is born on July 18 in Umtata, South Africa.
1927	Mandela's father dies.
1934	At age sixteen, Mandela participates in the traditional ceremony that signals the end of childhood. He first becomes aware of the oppression of blacks by South African whites .
1939	Mandela enters Fort Hare University
1944	Mandela marries Evelyn Mase.
1948	The Nationalist Party of South Africa is voted into power and begins to implement its policies of apartheid.
1952	Nelson Mandela opens his law practice with Oliver Tambo. It is the first black law practice in South Africa.
1956	Mandela is arrested after organizing a peaceful protest and is charged with treason.
1957	Mandela divorces his wife, Evelyn.
1958	Mandela marries Winnie Madikizela, a social worker.
1961	Mandela is found not guilty of treason.
1962	Mandela is arrested again and sentenced to five years in prison.
1964	Although already in prison, Mandela is sentenced to life in prison on another charge of sabotage and trying to overthrow the government.
1990	Nelson Mandela is finally released from prison after twenty-seven years.
1993	Nelson Mandela and former president F. W. de Clerk are awarded the Nobel Peace Prize.
1994	Mandela is elected the first black president of South Africa.
1996	Nelson and Winnie Mandela divorce.
1998	Mandela marries his third wife, Graca Machel, the widow of a former president of Mozambique.

Glossary

apartheid (uh-PART-hite)
Apartheid is a political policy of keeping races of people apart. South Africa lived under laws of apartheid for many years.

boycotting (BOY-kot-ting)
Boycotting is refusing to do business with a person or group to show that you don't approve of the way that they operate and to try to force them to change. Many countries boycotted businesses in South Africa because of apartheid.

dismantle (dis-MANT-uhl)
To dismantle means to take something apart. President de Klerk and Nelson Mandela worked to dismantle apartheid.

Dutch (DUCH)
The people, products, and language of the Netherlands are referred to as Dutch. Many Dutch people settled in South Africa.

folklore (FO-klor)
The stories, customs, and beliefs of a group of people that are passed down from generation to generation are called folklore. Mandela's tribe was rich in folklore.

magistrates (MAJ-uh-strayts)
Magistrates are local government officials who act as judges. For many years, all the magistrates in South Africa were white.

racist (RAY-sist)
A racist person or group believes that one group of people is better than another just because of the color of their skin. The policies of apartheid were racist.

sabotage (SAB-uh-tazh)
Sabotage is the deliberate damage or destruction of property. Mandela and the ANC chose to sabotage buildings as a way to hurt the South African government.

veld (VELT)
A veld is a large area of grassy land. The Tembu tribe relied on the veld for their cattle to survive.

Index

acquired immunodeficiency syndrome (AIDS), 35
African National Congress (ANC), 18, 19, 20, 21, 25, 26, 29, 32
Afrikaners, 20
apartheid laws, 20, 22, 29, 30, 35

boycotts, 29

Christianity, 12
de Clerk, F. W., 30, 31, 32

Dutch South Africans, 14, 20

gold mining, 13
Great Britain, 11, 14

Johannesburg, 15

Mandela, Graca Machel (wife), 35
Mandela, Nelson Rolihlahla
    arrest of, 21, 23
    birth of, 7
    childhood of, 9, 12
    education of, 9, 11, 14, 15, 17
    imprisonment of, 25, 29
    law career of, 15, 18, 19, 21
    as leader of Spear of the Nation league, 23
    marriage of, 15, 19, 26, 35
    as Nobel Peace Prize recipient, 31
    as president of South Africa, 35
    as president of ANC, 32
    as president of ANC youth league, 18

as president of South Africa, 32
    release from prison, 30–31
    religion of, 12
Mandela, Winnie (wife), 26–27, 35
Methodist Church, 12
mining, 13

Nationalist Party, 20, 29, 30
Native passes, 19
Nobel Peace Prize, 31

sabotage, 23
Sisulu, Walter, 15, 18
South Africa
    government of, 7, 11, 12, 14, 20, 23, 30, 31, 32
    laws of, 12, 13, 17, 18, 19, 20, 22, 29, 30, 35
Spear of the Nation league, 23

Tambo, Oliver, 18
Tembu people, 7, 9, 17, 23
Tembuland, 7
Transvaal province, 15

University College of Fort Hare, 14

voting rights, 32

Witwatersrand University, 17

Xhosa language, 7

For Further Reading

Books

Adi, Hakim. *Nelson Mandela: Father of Freedom.* Orlando, Fla.: Raintree/Steck Vaughn, 2001.

Connolly, Sean. *Nelson Mandela: An Unauthorized Biography.* Chicago: Heinemann Library, 2000.

Mandela, Nelson. *Long Walk to Freedom: The Autobiography of Nelson Mandela.* Boston: Little, Brown, 1994.

Peoples of Africa, vols. 1-11. New York: Marshall Cavendish, 2001.

Web Sites

Visit our homepage for lots of links about Nelson Mandela:
http://www.childsworld.com/links.html

Note to Parents, Teachers, and Librarians:
We routinely verify our Web links to make sure they're safe,
active sites—so encourage your readers to check them out!

About the Author

Robert Green earned a bachelor's degree in English literature from Boston University and a master's degree in journalism from New York University. He has also studied Chinese on a Blakemore Foundation Language Grant in Taiwan.

Green is the author of nineteen other nonfiction books for young adults, including *Modern Nations of the World: China* and *Modern Nations of the World: Taiwan* and biographies of Caesar, Cleopatra, Alexander the Great, Tutankhamun, Herod the Great, and Hannibal.